A Special Gift

PRESENTED TO

FROM

DATE

A LASTING LEGACY
FOR YOUR CHILDREN

A FATHER'S
Heritage

Your Life Story
in Your Own Words

COUNTRYMAN

Nashville, Tennessee

www.jcountryman.com

Design: Koechel Peterson & Associates, Inc., Minneapolis, MN

ISBN: 1-4041-01659

Printed and bound in the United States

INTRODUCTION

"What grade did you get in high school English, Dad?" "What did you do on your first date?" Sound familiar? Your son or daughter has probably asked these questions and many more. Why? Curiosity partly, but mostly because they care—about you. They want to know what you did when you were growing up because they want to know you.

That is the purpose of this book, which is a book about you—your family history, your childhood memories, humorous incidents, and meaningful traditions from your life. It is a personal biography just waiting to be written. Yes, there are planes to catch, meetings to attend, grass to mow, and the car to wash, but those are not a legacy you can pass on to your child. This book is.

Presented in a twelve-month format, this journal provides an array of questions your son or daughter might ask with space for your answers. Questions like, "Describe the most fun you ever had on a Fourth of July." Or "When you went to a ball game as a boy, what kind of food did you eat?" Or "What is the nicest thing you ever did for your mother and father?"

These questions will help you write down the special memories, thoughts, and ideas you want to share with your children. You may choose to complete the journal in a few days, a few weeks, or throughout the course of the year. When you have filled in all of the pages you will have a loving memoir—a spiritual legacy—to pass on to your children. They will cherish this book about you for a lifetime.

This book is for fathers of all ages, because it is never too early or too late to share your life with those you love. May *A Father's Heritage* draw you closer to your children as you share this memoir of your life . . . straight from your heart to theirs.

PERSONAL
Portrait

your full given name ....

your date of birth ....

your place of birth ....

your mother's full name ....

the place and date of her birth ....

....

your father's full name ....

the place and date of his birth ....

....

the names of your paternal grandparents ....

....

the places and dates of their births ....

....

....

the names of your maternal grandparents ....

....

....

the places and dates of their births ....

....

....

the names of your siblings

the places and dates of their births

the date and place of your marriage

the full given name of your wife

the names and birth dates of your children

What is
YOUR FAVORITE

sport

book

leisure activity

dessert

author

Scripture, saying, or quotation

hymn or song

vacation spot

type of food

sports team

FAVORITE

PHOTO

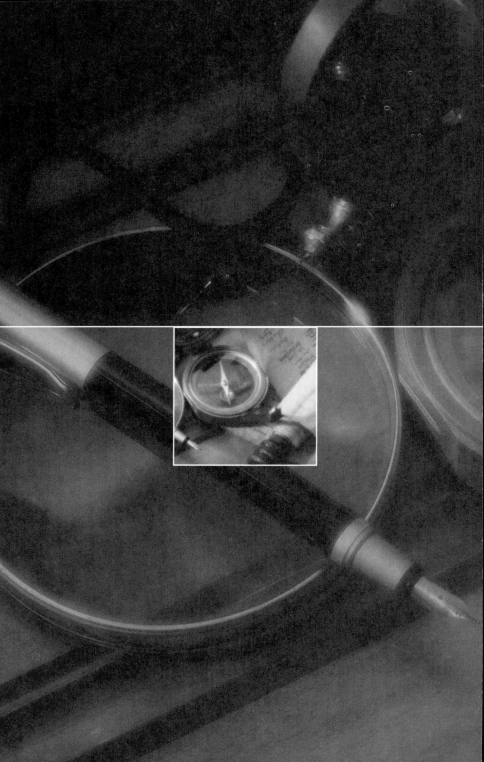

JANUARY

*O*ur stories
are inextricably interwoven.
What you do is part of my story;
what I do is part of yours.

Daniel Taylor

What did you enjoy
doing most as a child?

Did you prefer
doing it alone or
with someone else?

January

Who gave you

your name and why?

Did you have a nickname? How did you get it?

Describe your childhood home.

What was your favorite room?

What was the silliest thing

you ever did?

How old were you?

What were Sundays like as a child? ....

Did you go to church? ....

Visit grandparents? ....

Was there a family dinner? ....

If so, what was a typical menu? ....

....

....

....

....

....

....

....

....

....

....

....

ther's
HERITAGE

Where did your father go to work
every day and what did he do?

Did his work interest you?

Did your mother have a job
or did she work at home?

What was your favorite sport

or outdoor activity?

Why was this your favorite?

Did you have a favorite bedtime
story or a prayer that you said
before you went to sleep?

Who tucked you in?

23

Where was your

childhood home located?

Did you enjoy living there?

Describe your grandparents.

What did you enjoy

most about them?

Can you remember being afraid as a boy?
What was your greatest fear?

How did you deal with it?

January

Recall for me five
of the most important
lessons you have
learned in life

Father's
HERITAGE

FEBRUARY

GRATITUDE IS THE

MEMORY OF THE HEART.

Massieu

Can you recall an
especially interesting
visitor to your home?

What made that person or the occasion memorable?

What did you want to be _____

"when you grew up?" _____

_____

_____

_____

_____

_____

How old were you? _____

_____

Did that change over the years? _____

_____

_____

_____

_____

_____

_____

_____

31

Describe the most memorable
Valentine you ever received.
Who sent it to you?

How far did you have to travel
to attend elementary, junior high,
and high school, and how
did you get there?

33

Do you remember a special book from your childhood?
A Bible? A storybook?

Who gave it to you?

Do you still have it?

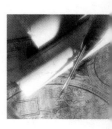

As young boy, did you participate in church, scouting, or some other organization or activity?

How important a role did that play in your life?

Did you go to ball games as a boy?

What kind of food did you eat?

When you were growing up, did you have any animals?

What were their names?

Was it important to you to have a pet?

Tell me about your mother's cooking.

Can you recall your favorite meal?

What made it your favorite?

Did you ever get into fights with other kids?

Did you ever start a fight?

Or stop one?

What chores did you have to
do when you were growing up?

Did you get
an allowance?
How much was it?

February

Who gave you your first job?

What kind of job was it?

How much money did you make?

Share your idea of

what makes a good friend.

February

MARCH

WE HAVE ONE LIFE TO LIVE—

AND ONE CHANCE TO LIVE IT

IN THE RICHEST WAY POSSIBLE.

Judith Thurman

Tell about an award or honor
_____

or special recognition
_____

you have received.
_____

_____

_____

_____

_____

_____

_____

_____

_____

_____

_____

_____

_____

_____

_____

_____

_____

Describe your favorite
pastime or hobby as a child.

Father's
HERITAGE

What mischievous prank did
you pull on someone?

How did it affect you?

Did you have a television
when you were growing up?

What was your
favorite program?
Why?

What were some crazy fads

from your school days?

Did you participate in them?

Why or why not?

Who was your favorite teacher?

How did that teacher

influence your life?

51

Did you ever have a special

hideaway or clubhouse?

Describe it for me.

In high school, what extracurricular
activities did you enjoy most?

Why did you choose those activities?

What is the nicest thing you
ever did for your mother and father?

Did you admire a famous person?

What made that person admirable?

When did you have

your first date?

Tell me about it.

What do you remember

about your first kiss?

March

Share some of your

insights for working

well with others.

APRIL

*I*T IS IN THE SHELTER

OF EACH OTHER

THAT THE PEOPLE LIVE.

Irish Proverb

Did you enjoy reading as a boy?

What were some of the most
memorable books you read?

April

What were your family finances
like when you were growing up?
How did that affect you?

What individuals have had
the greatest impact on your life?
In what ways?

When did you first
learn about sex?

Would you
recommend the
same for young
people today?
Why or why not?

As a teenager did you rebel

or do things your parents

wouldn't have approved of?

How do you feel about that now?

Father's
HERITAGE

List three things you wish you
had done during your junior high
and high school years, but didn't.

April

What did your family ....

like to do on weekends? ....

....

....

....

....

....

Describe one particularly memorable one.

....

....

....

....

....

....

....

....

During childhood,

who was your best friend?

Share some of your fondest

memories of fun times together.

What is your favorite memory
of your mother?

Why is it so

special to you?

Did you ever keep a scrapbook

of photos, autographs,

or memories of special occasions?

Describe what this meant to you.

What image of your father
is the most striking in your memory?

Why that image?

List one special memory

about each of your

brothers and sisters.

Share with me your

father's attitude toward life

and how that affected you.

April

MAY

W

WHO,

BEING LOVED,

IS POOR?

Oscar Wilde

May

If you were to find an old toy box
in your attic, what toys would you
remember most fondly?

Why?

Father's
HERITAGE

What is one of the most
difficult choices you ever
had to make?
Would you make the
same choice again?

Do you remember a time
when you felt particularly
unsure or confused?
What did you do?

What kind of car did your family drive?

Were you proud of it
or embarrassed by it?

Why?

How often did
your family go to church?

What pastor or Sunday school teacher
do you remember most?

How did that person influence you?

Did you ever go to a dance?
Tell me about it.

May

Did your family attend

family reunions?

What activities did

everyone enjoy?

Tell me about your

favorite cousins,

aunts, or uncles.

When you were young,

did you ever go to a funeral?

How did that affect you?

If you had brothers and sisters,

did you feel your parents

treated you all the same?

Why or why not?

If you were an only child,

did you wish for

brothers and sisters?

Why?

May

Did your high school have college or career days? ....

What field interested you most? ....

....

....

....

....

....

....

....

What did you want to become ....

when you grew up? ....

....

....

....

....

....

....

May

If you went to college
or to a career training school,
where did you go and why?

Where did you live when you were going to college or developing a career?

Describe an unforgettable experience
from that time in your life.

Are there certain
Scriptures or other
writings that you
repeatedly turn to for
inspiration or guidance?

JUNE

*T*HE LINKING OF GENERATIONS,

THE HISTORICAL LINEAGE OF FAMILY,

THE SHARING OF LOVE . . .

GIVE PURPOSE TO LIFE.

George Landberg

What were your youthful goals
and ambitions for life?

Which ones have you

been able to fulfill?

If you learned to play a musical instrument,

tell me your memories of lessons, practice,

and your music teacher.

If not, what instrument did

you want to play and why?

How old were you

when you met Mom?

What attracted you to her?

June

When did you know that Mom was
the "one and only one" for you?
How did you know?

Father's
HERITAGE

Share a memory
about the way you
proposed to Mom.

Tell me about your wedding day.

What happened? How did you feel?

Were you nervous, scared, happy?

Where did you go
on your honeymoon?

Describe at least one
humorous thing that
happened to you and Mom.

Do you remember the first meals

Mom cooked for you?

Do you dare comment on them?

Describe where you and Mom
lived after you got married.

What was the view like
from the kitchen window?

101

When did you and Mom
start talking about having children?
Why did you want children—or did you?

If you could go anywhere in the world on a second honeymoon, where would you go? Why?

What do you love best

about Mom now?

June

Record here your ideas on what
it takes for a husband and wife
to maintain a healthy marriage.

JULY

SOMEHOW, YEAR AFTER YEAR,

DAD MANAGED TO TAKE US ON VACATIONS

HE COULDN'T AFFORD TO PROVIDE,

IN ORDER TO MAKE MEMORIES THAT

WE COULDN'T AFFORD TO BE WITHOUT.

Ridhard Exley

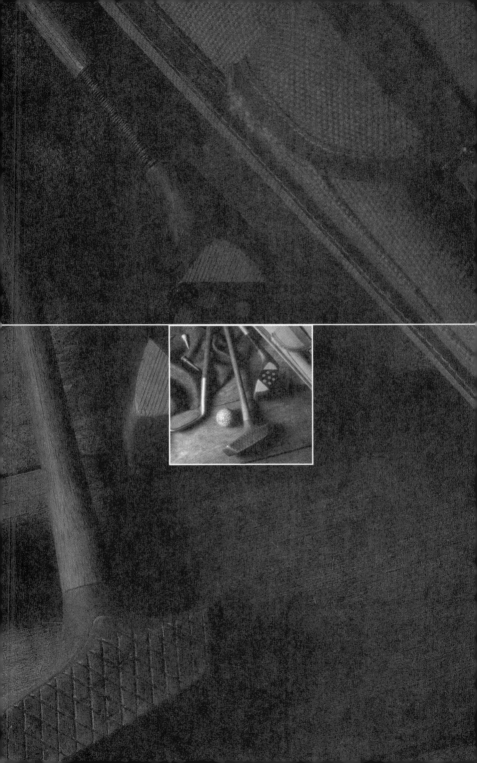

Tell me about your family summer

outings when you were young.

Did you go camping? Fishing? Swimming?

109

July

Describe the most fun you
ever had on a Fourth of July.

Did you ever
travel abroad?
How old were
you and where
did you go?

Who is the most ....

interesting foreigner ....

you have ever met? ....

....

....

What did this person help you ....

learn about his or her culture? ....

....

....

....

....

....

....

....

....

....

....

If you served in the armed forces,

describe how your time

in the service affected your life.

If you did not serve,

how did this affect your life?

Have you ever believed so strongly
in a cause that you marched
in a rally or demonstrated in protest?

What was the cause?

Why was it important to you?

July

What is the gutsiest thing you

ever did in your life?

Why did you do it?

Father's
HERITAGE

Where do you stand politically?
Do you lean toward
the left or the right?

Who, if anyone, has most greatly influenced
your current political views?

Did a tragedy ever

strike your family?

If so, how did it

affect you?

What is the best movie
you've ever seen?

If you could play one of the
characters in the film,
whom would you choose, and why?

How would you

finish this sentence?

"One thing my dad always said was . . ."

Did you ever go to summer camp?

Camping with the Boy Scouts?

Share one unforgettable memory.

July

Share a favorite poem,

passage of writing, or some

quotes that have been especially

meaningful in your life.

AUGUST

WHEN I COME HOME

FROM WORK AND SEE

THOSE LITTLE NOSES PRESSED

AGAINST THE WINDOW PANE,

THEN I KNOW I AM A SUCCESS.

Paul Faulkner

Is there any one book or author who
helped you to develop a philosophy of life?
Share some of those insights.

August

How have your
ideas about God
changed from when
you were young?

What kind of outdoor

work do you enjoy?

What kind do you dislike?

Father's
HERITAGE

What is your favorite

way to spend a day of leisure?

August

When did you learn how
to ride a bike, or to water ski,
snow ski, roller skate, or sail?
Share your memories of the experience.

Did you ever milk a cow or spend time
on a farm or in the country?
Tell me about it.

What places in the

world would you still

like to visit? Why?

Is there any childhood fear

that still haunts you?

How do you deal with this fear?

How do you enjoy helping people?
Share about a time when you
helped someone in need.

If you could carve one more

face on Mt. Rushmore,

whose face would it be? Why?

In what ways are you like
your mother?

Like your father?

Looking back in life,
what one thing would you
have done differently?

Why?

August

Share some tips

for a great vacation.

SEPTEMBER

WHAT LIES BEHIND US

AND WHAT LIES BEFORE US

ARE TINY MATTERS

COMPARED TO WHAT

LIES WITHIN US.

Ralph Waldo Emerson

Tell about a special outing
you took with your dad.

Father's
HERITAGE

What makes this a poignant
memory for you?

September

Did you learn mechanics

or woodworking as a young person?

How and when?

What were some of

your most memorable projects?

142

September

As a young person did you
volunteer for work in church,
community, or social services?
Tell me about it.

When did you move away from home?
Describe where you lived
and how you felt about it.

September

Tell me about some
of your closest friends
after you and Mom
got married.

What were some of
the fun things you
would do together?

What is something
you learned from
an especially difficult
time in your life?

What is something you
learned from an especially
happy time in your life?

What special talents

did your parents nurture in you?

How have you developed those talents?

What would you

still like to learn to do?

Why?

What did you enjoy
doing with your mom?
Share a special time with her.

September

How would you
describe yourself:
tender-hearted or
tough-minded?

If you were to write
a book about Mom,
how would you
title the book?
The first few chapters?

How do you describe

"success"?

OCTOBER

*L*IFE'S JOURNEY IS CURCULAR.

IT APPEARS THE YEARS DON'T

CARRY US AWAY FROM OUR FATHER—

THEY RETURN US TO THEM.

Michel Marriott

If you could have two hours
of conversation with anyone on earth,
who would that be?

Why that person?

What would you talk about?

Father's
HERITAGE

Who are some of the best public speakers
you have ever heard?

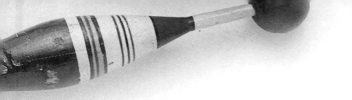

Why did they
impress you?

159

October

How would you like

to be remembered?

Why is this important to you?

Share a hilarious travel experience.

What do you consider

to be some of life's

most difficult challenges?

October

Have you ever been in an accident,

had surgery or a long illness?

How did this affect your outlook on life?

Do you have a favorite sports team?
Why is that one your favorite?

October

What responsibilities
did your parents
require of you as a
child?

How did this affect
your growth and
development?
How you raised
your children?

What is the most
frightening thing
that has ever
happened to you?
How did you handle the experience?

What do you consider

to be life's greatest gifts?

When and where did you buy

your first house or piece of real estate?

Describe the significance this held for you.

Share some of your ideas on
how to develop and maintain
good physical health.

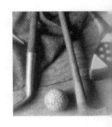

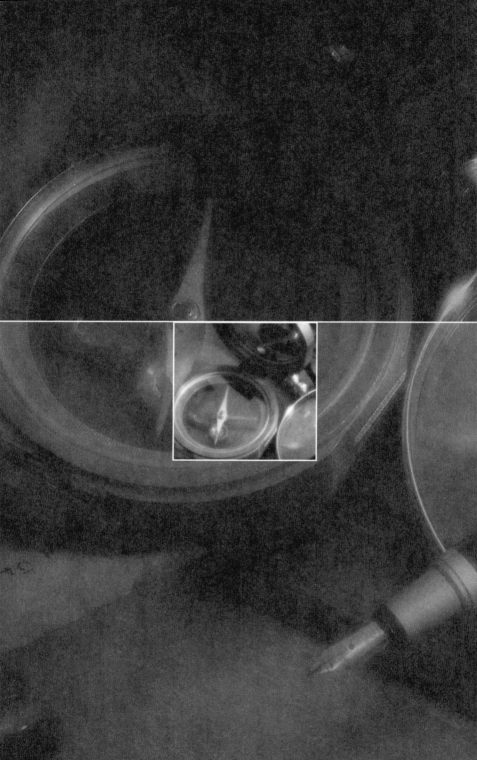

NOVEMBER

GOD CALLS

EACH GENERATION

TO PASS DOWN

SPIRITUAL TRUTH

TO THE NEXT.

Dennis Rainey

As a teenager, did you belong
to a club or church youth group?

Tell me about the individuals in the group
who were most significant to you.

What is your most
treasured possession
and why?

Who were your male
role models when
you were growing up?
How have they affected the kind of person you are?

What two people have made
the greatest spiritual impact on your life?

What made them so significant to you?

When you were a new father,

what was your greatest fear?

Your greatest joy?

What is your most

vivid memory about

my childhood?

What would you change
about my childhood if you could?

Father's
HERITAGE

Describe a fond
Thanksgiving memory.
What makes this
special to you?

What are some
things from your
childhood that
you are thankful for?

What childhood memory first comes

to mind when you think about winter?

How do you respond to that memory?

Describe the most interesting

person you ever met.

What were the qualities that

made that individual so outstanding?

What family customs or traditions would you like to pass
on to your children and grandchildren?
Why are they important to you?

Tell me what four things
you would never leave
behind on a trip and
explain why.

DECEMBER

*T*HOSE WHO LOVED YOU

AND WERE HELPED BY YOU

WILL REMEMBER YOU.

SO CARVE YOUR NAME ON

HEARTS AND NOT ON MARBLE.

C. H. Spurgeon

Describe some Christmas traditions
from your childhood and tell how
they have influenced your life.

Were you ever in a Christmas program? ....

....

.... ² ......

How did you respond to the experience? ....

....

....

....

....

....

....

....

....

....

....

....

....

....

....

What is the best Christmas present

you ever received?

Why was that the best?

Tell about a memorable

Christmas visit with relatives.

What is your favorite
Christmas carol? ....

....

....

Why? ....

....

....

....

....

....

....

....

....

....

....

....

....

....

....

What would be

the most wonderful

gift you could receive?

Why?

What would you like to see happen
in the next ten years in your life?

December

In the world?

Father's
HERITAGE

What have people older than
you taught you about life?

What have you learned from
children and young people?

As you look back in life, name three
of the most fantastic changes that
have taken place in the world.
How have these affected your life?

197

Where would you still like to go
and what would you like to do
once you got there?

What is your favorite way

    to spend a rainy day?

What word best describes your life?

Explain why.

What advice about life

do you want others to remember?

Notes

Father's
HERITAGE

NOTES

PHOTOS